THE FIRE
OF
GOD'S LOVE

A
GLIMPSE
OF
HEAVEN

© Efstathiadis Group 2004

ISBN: 960-226-608-2

EFSTATHIADIS GROUP S.A.
88 Drakontos Str.,
104 42 Athens
tel.: ++3210 5154 650,
fax: ++3210 5154 657
e-mail: efgroup@otenet.gr
GREECE

Printed and bound in Greece

Cover desigh: Patti Gialerakis and Elina Logotheti.
*Photographs: Photographs are mostly by the author and friends. The
photos at pages: 114, 116, 121, 142, 152 and 154 are reproduced by
kind permission of the* «**Anatoli**» *newspaper of Aghios Nikolaos, Crete
with the help of Michalis Kosiris.*

A GLIMPSE OF HEAVEN

An introduction
to
Greek Orthodox Churches
and
Worship for Visitors

by

Chris Moorey

To Fr. Michalis and Fr. Panagiotis
who gently and lovingly guided us
into the Orthodox Church.

Στον Πατέρα Μιχάλη και στον Πατέρα Παναγιώτη
που με ευγένεια και αγάπη μας οδήγησαν
στην Ορθόδοξη Εκκλησία.

Contents

INTRODUCTION

No visitor to Greece, even those who come just for the sun in the day and the wine at night,can fail to notice the important part played by religion in this country. There seems to be a church on every corner, their density exceeding even Norwich, England, which is reputed to have had until recently 52 churches, one for every Sunday of the year*. Everywhere along the roadside one can see small shrines shaped like churches, while religious celebrations and processions are a common sight even in the most remote villages. Every taxi and bus has its share of small icons and crosses hang-

It is also reputed to have had 365 pubs, but that's another story!

ing from the rear view mirror and you can see the local people crossing themselves whenever they pass a church. In fact, one of the most hair-raising experiences I have had in Greece was in a taxi going round a sharp bend with a church on the corner. The taxi driver, who already had his left hand occupied with a mobile phone, then took his right hand off the wheel to cross himself!

So, what is it all about? Are the Greek people more religious than other nations? I don't think most Greeks would claim to be holier than their western or northern European cousins but it is a fact that the Church and religious rites play a much greater part in their lives than has been seen in many countries for at least a century.

Although the Orthodox Church exists in many countries of the world, it is still largely unknown to most tourists and when my wife and I first came to Greece, being naturally inquisitive, we found we were for ever asking questions: Why are the churches full of icons and short of seating? Why don't the priests cut their hair? What are those little roadside shrines for? Why is Easter a different date in Greece? Now, after some years, I am able to answer these and other questions and feel that perhaps the answers may be of interest to visitors who are equally curious and want to understand the country beyond the level of bouzouki and souvlaki*.

This book is meant to be primarily factual and descriptive but the furnishings and decorations of the churches, the services and other rites are all so intricately intermingled with Orthodox theology that I will need to discuss some of the beliefs of Orthodoxy, even if in a very superficial way. However, this is neither an attempt to summarise the doctrines of Orthodoxy, nor a treatise on iconography or the Orthodox liturgy. On all these subjects innumerable brilliant books have been written and, if your interest is awakened, I have suggested some excellent further reading at the end of this book. This is more a "tourist guidebook", not to a series of cities or archaeological sites but to a way of life and a system of beliefs. If it makes your sightseeing a little more interesting and informed, it has achieved its object, but I hope that it will also give you a greater understanding of your Greek hosts. If it makes you want to find out more about Orthodoxy, so much the better.

Although this has been written for visitors to Greece, much of it is true of Russian and other Orthodox churches.

...come in **all** shapes and sizes...

...and can sometimes be found in the strangest places,

including caves and under multi-storey office blocks

16

CHURCHES

General Appearance

One is sometimes surprised by the sheer number of churches in Greece and wonders what size of congregation needs so many. The answer is that they don't. While every village and town has its main church, many other churches are only used on a few days (sometimes only once) a year. Some of these are very old, where the village has outgrown the original church and a new larger one has been built. Many, however, have been built by individuals, either as thanks for answered prayers, as voluntary penance for sins, in memory of a departed loved one or simply as acts of piety. This practice,

Chris Moorey

common in western Europe in previous times, is still
a living part of Greek culture. In my own village, no
less than three churches have been built by individuals in the last few years: one was a thanks offering for
a child's recovery from a life-threatening illness; the
second was the rebuilding of a very old chapel, fallen
into disrepair; the other one was built as the fulfil-
ment of a vow made as a very young man.

In spite of their number, every single church in
Greece, even the tiniest chapel, is used at least once a
year on the feast day of its patron saint. Services on
these days are very popular and, since the churches
are very small, most of the congregation sit or stand
outside and much of the service takes place in front of
the church (a sort of open air nave). On summer days,
these occasions can be extremely pleasant and, as
always in Greece, the opportunity for a picnic and party
afterwards. For the same reason, these little churches
are popular for summer baptisms and weddings.

There are three main patterns in Greek churches. The smaller churches and chapels are simple
rectangles with the altar at the east end and a portico
at the west. This was the style of the earliest Christian
churches and many of this type are of great age. Secondly, the larger churches and cathedrals are often

also rectangular but with two (or more rarely, three) aisles. Many monastic churches use this style. Finally, there is the style, familiar from countless postcards and ornaments: the cross-shaped church with a central dome. This "Byzantine style" is based on the great Church of Holy Wisdom (Saint Sophia) built in Constantinople in 522AD and could be called the typically Greek style.

All Orthodox churches (like Anglican and Roman Catholic) are either named after a saint or the Virgin Mary or bear the name of the Holy Spirit, Holy Trinity or one of the great feasts of the church - Transfiguration, Annunciation etc. However, the churches with a double aisle are dedicated to two saints, one for each aisle*. Thus, for example, a church may be "The Church of St. Nicholas and the Holy Spirit". Some of the larger domed churches also have side chapels dedicated to saints other than the "main" one.

A rare, possibly unique, use of the double aisled church can be found in the tiny church, now disused, on the island of Spinalonga near Elounda in Crete. During the Venetian occupation of Crete in the 13th to 17th centuries, one aisle was used by the Venetian Catholics and the other by the local Orthodox Greeks, an example of religious tolerance rare for that period (or any other, perhaps).

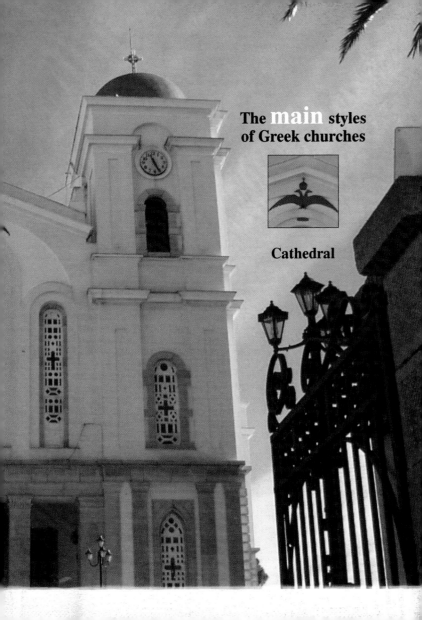

The **main** styles
of Greek churches

Cathedral

Two aisles

Simple

Byzantine

Three aisles

Exterior

The outside of all Christian churches is design-ed to be pleasing to the eye but the beauty of Greek churches lies mainly in their simplici-ty. Unlike western European churches and cathed-rals, there is little in the way of embellishment: no buttresses, spires or carvings and certainly no statues*. It is rare to find even the additional cupolas which are such a feature of the Russian Orthodox style. Instead, we see clean lines and plain colours, white, cream or beige for the building, red or blue for the roof. The only ornamentation is the cross.

Attached to the church, or very near it, is the BELL TOWER and here a greater variety of artistic expres-sion can be seen. Many are simple and functional but some feature elaborately carved openings and intricate decoration and are often of great beauty. This indicates the importance attached to bells in the Orthodox Church.

As in all Christian churches, the BELLS serve a double purpose. They are rung as expressions of joy

---

* *There is no prohibition against statues in the Ortho-dox Church but by very strong tradition they have very rarely been used.*

on feast days, weddings and other great occasions and tolled as expressions of mourning for funerals. Primarily, however, they act as a call to the faithful to summon them to worship. In rural communities, where time has its own, usually slower, rhythm, it is quite common for the exact times of services to vary. In this situation, the sound of bells becomes a more reliable indication of the start of a service than a watch. Certainly, anyone living or staying close to a church in Greece has little chance of a lie in on Sunday mornings. Once the bells start ringing to indicate the beginning of the service even those who are not able to attend, wherever they are, will cross themselves, identifying themselves with the worshippers, at least in spirit. In my first year as a teacher in Greece, I found it a little disconcerting to suddenly find the whole class crossing themselves in the middle of a lesson. Now I have got used to it and realise that perhaps it isn't a bad idea to occasionally be reminded that there may be more important things in life than school or work.

On feast days or when the bishop is present, the exterior of the church is often decorated with FLAGS, usually the Greek national flag and a yellow flag bearing a black, two-headed eagle. This is the emblem of the Greek Orthodox Church and originates from the Byzantine imperial flag*. The decoration is completed by lines of pennants featuring Christian symbols or short scriptural texts.

Etiquette

Visitors and tourists are quite welcome to look around Orthodox churches, although sadly the scourge of vandalism and theft has even hit Greece and many churches are locked when not in use. However, most of the larger churches are open during the day in the main season and, for the determined, a key to the locked churches is usually available nearby. Ask at the nearest kiosk or cafeneion and somebody will probably be able to help.

When entering a church, even when there is no service, visitors are expected to show respect for the beliefs of the faithful. Beach wear, shorts or very short skirts are distinctly frowned on and, although

---

* *The two-headed eagle was also the emblem of Tsarist Russia, which considered itself to be the continuation of the Byzantine Christian Empire after the fall of Constantinople in 1453. In fact, Moscow was often called The Third Rome.*

most Greeks, even the priests, show a remarkable tolerance towards the eccentricities of visitors, don't be surprised to be shouted at or even chased out by an angry cleric if you enter the church in a bikini!

Photography and filming are generally allowed unless there is a service in progress but it is best to ask permission, if possible, especially in old churches where there may be delicate frescoes or icons. It is strictly forbidden to take photos or film during services without the prior permission of the priest or on "family occasions" such as weddings or baptisms.

BELLTOWERS
AND
FLAGS

**Joy lies at the heart
of Orthodoxy,
*"Let the heavens rejoice
and let the earth be glad"***

Interior

Each church, whatever its size, has three sections, reflecting the three orders of Christians in the early Church: those awaiting baptism, the baptized faithful and the clergy.

The PORTICO (Narthex) at the entrance to the church was originally the area where the non-baptized stood as onlookers but not participants in the holy rites. This use is now largely vestigial as most Orthodox in Greece are baptised as infants and Orthodox churches generally welcome non-Orthodox visitors to their services. However, the portico, is still used occasionally for parts of the baptism and marriage services, as well as helping to keep out the draughts in winter.

The largest area of the church is the NAVE (Kyrios Naos). This is where the congregation stand during services and where baptisms, weddings, funerals, memorial services and parts of other services take place.

Steps from the Nave lead up to a raised area in front of a wooden or marble screen, richly decorated with icons and called the ICONOSTASIS. This divides the nave from the SANCTUARY (Ieron Vima) in which the altar stands and where the priest conducts the Communion service and many other rites of the Church. The sanctuary is elevated from the rest of the church ("Vima" means "rostrum") both for symbolic reasons, being a stairway towards Heaven, and for the more mundane reason of making the priest more audible and visible to the congregation*. Entry into the sanctuary is strictly forbidden except for clergy, altar boys or other people with specific duties.

---

* *Most modern churches, however, make full use of microphones so that the service is not only audible within the church but relayed through loud speakers outside as well. This has the added convenience that the old men in the nearby cafeneions can follow the service in comfort.*

General **view** of church

GENERAL LAYOUT
OF TYPICAL
BYZANTINE CHURCH

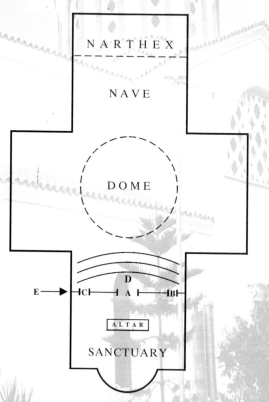

NARTHEX

NAVE

DOME

D

E → ⊢C⊢ ⊢ A ⊢ ⊢B⊢

ALTAR

SANCTUARY

A - *ROYAL GATE* **B** - *DOOR TO PROTHESIS*
C - *DOOR TO DIAKONIKON* **D** - *STEPS* **E** - *ICONOSTASIS*

GENERAL LAYOUT
OF CHURCH WITH
TWO AISLES

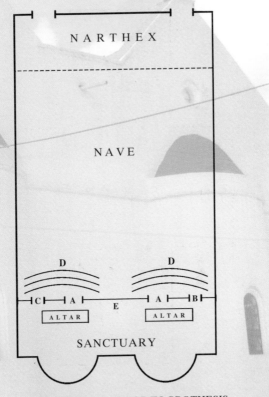

NARTHEX

NAVE

D   D

C A   E   A B

ALTAR   ALTAR

SANCTUARY

A - *ROYAL GATE* **B** - *DOOR TO PROTHESIS*
C - *DOOR TO DIAKONIKON* **D** - *STEPS* **E** - *ICONOSTASIS*

ICONS

The first thing that strikes most visitors to an Orthodox church are the number of icons. The church is full of representations of the saints, either as framed paintings, as mosaics or as frescoes. The walls and even the ceilings are often a solid mass of colour, creating an impression of tremendous beauty. And yet, beauty is not the only, or even primary, purpose of the icons. Icons are of such fundamental theological significance in Orthodoxy that although various emperors in the 8th and 9th centuries attempted to forbid them, their restoration in 834 A.D is still commemorated in a special celebration on the first Sunday of Lent, called revealingly "The Triumph of Orthodoxy".

The word "icon" is simply the Greek word for "picture" and, without going into deep theology and at the risk of gross over-simplification, one can say that icons are basically representations of the saints designed to make them real to us. Just as we keep photos of our loved ones, especially our family, in our homes, so in the church the Orthodox keep pictures of their loved ones in the Christian family: Christ, the Virgin Mary, the angels and the saints. Just as we will sometimes kiss a photo of a loved one, especially one who has passed on, so the Orthodox will kiss an icon as a sign of respect and love. Deep respect is shown to Christ and the Mother of God by kissing the hand, while love for members of the Christian family is expressed by kissing icons of the saints on the face. Note that the Orthodox do not "worship" icons (worship is reserved for God) but they do show reverence towards the life of the saint depicted and honour his or her holiness.

Icons are representations but they are not portraits. Although they are recognizably human, at the same time, they do not seem quite real. The stylized nature of the icons is quite deliberate and based on sound theological principles. Most Christians believe in the ultimate resurrection of the body and, although the Orthodox church generally maintains a "reverent agnosticism" about the precise nature of this bodily resurrection, it is certain that the body will not be exactly the same "fallen" body as we now possess but a body in some way transfigured and showing outwardly the spirituality within. It is this transfigured body that the icons attempt to symbolize*.

On the other hand, although the pictures are stylized, one can see clearly the individuality of the humans represented. Many of them, especially the later saints, have been reproduced down the ages from actual knowledge of the person. Indeed, it has been argued with some evidence that even some of the representations of the apostles, Peter and Paul in particular, are based on contemporaneous portraits. What is certain is that, while the saints have their sanctity in common, their humanity differentiates them. Some look stern, even fierce, reminding us that not all holy people are easy to live with**. From

---

* It was his early training as an icon painter that helped to form El Greco's "otherworldly"and ethereal style.

** Those who have been at the receiving end of Mother Theresa's tongue have vouched for this.

the eyes of others love and tenderness shine out. Occasionally one can even see a distinct twinkle in the eye. These are real people portrayed.

The range of icons to be seen in the different churches makes it impossible to do more than give a few general comments about the icons themselves. Most guide books to individual churches or areas will give details. In describing the location of icons in various parts of the church, I have followed the "classical" plan developed in Russia and now common throughout the Orthodox world. However, there are wide variations in the details in different churches.

As you explore Orthodox churches, you will find an enormous range of icons but the main types are as follows. Most common, of course, are icons of Christ or the Virgin Mary or of individual saints. You will also see composites of a number of saints who are related in some way; for example, all the martyrs from a particular area or for a particular month, the fathers of the church etc. Scenes from the Bible, particularly the life of Christ, or from the lives of the saints are also common. Finally, there are what could be called "hymns of praise". These are composite pictures illustrating a particular theme often based on one of the Orthodox hymns. For example, an icon in the Topkapi Monastery in western Crete, called "Lord Thou Art Great" includes 61 vignettes based on the prayer said at Epiphany (Theophania), showing examples of God's greatness and mercy from the Garden of Eden to the Ascension of Christ. These "hymns" are often of great beauty and interest and, in artistic terms, rival Breughel in their complex detail. One can literally spend hours studying them.

Not only are the figures in icons stylized, but the colours, the clothing, and the various objects worn or held by the saints are also stylized and symbolic. For example, martyrs are depicted holding a small cross*, while doctors of the church and eminent theologians carry a book or a scroll; emperors and empresses wear a crown and bishops raise one hand in blessing while the other holds the gospel. Note that, unlike western religious paintings, the martyrs are rarely shown with symbols of their martyrdom as more

Note, however, that St. Helen is always shown holding a life-size cross not as a symbol of martyrdom but because she is reputed to have found the relics of the actual cross of the crucifixion. It is certainly true that, in her pilgrimage in search of the cross, she founded many of the churches that still exist in the Holy Land. Along with her son, the Emperor Constantine, she is called "Equal to the Apostles" in recognition of their role in bringing the Roman Empire to Christianity.

importance is attached to what they died for rather than the means, often gruesome, of their death.

Because of the symbolism and spiritual importance of icons, the icon painter requires not only artistic ability but a detailed knowledge of tradition coupled with a spiritual attitude to his work. However, the art of icon painting is not a dead art of copying and repetition. In spite of the stylization, there is scope for individual inspiration and there are many quite distinct schools of icon painting. Moreover, there are still fine icon painters who, while respecting the traditions, have created icons for the modern mind.

The names of the saints are always written on the icon and, if you have some knowledge of the Greek alphabet, it is usually possible to work out who it is. There are some notes to help you plus the complete Greek Alphabet in Appendix 2.

The Holy Trinity - mosaic

Christ the Almighty

The Virgin Mary, Mother of God

The Virgin Mary - mosaic

ὁ ἅγ(ιος)

ΜΕΤΑΝΟ
ΕΙΤΕ·
ΗΓΓΙΚΕ
ΓΑΡΗΒΑ
ΣΙΛΕΙΑ
ΤΩΝΟΥ
ΡΑΝΩΝ

John the Baptist,
the Forerunner

Icons are painted in a symbolic style to represent the transfigured body after resurrection...

Ss. Constantine and Eleni

IC XC   NIKOΛAOC

St. Nicholas

...but it is possible that representations of Ss. Peter and Paul are based on Roman medallions made shortly after their deaths.

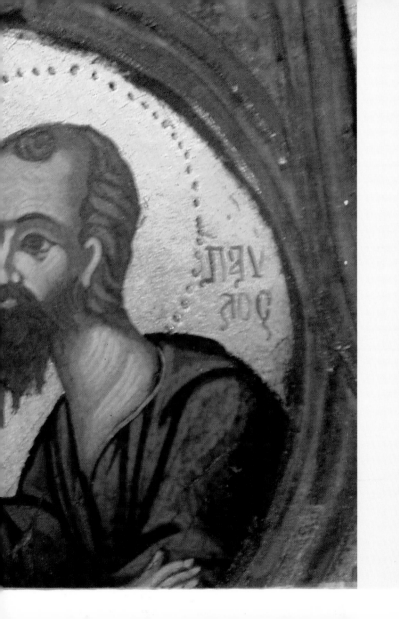

However stylized, icons clearly show the humanity of the saints as well as their spirituality

In this detail from *O Lord, Thou art Great* (Toplou Monastery, Crete), the Virgin Mary seems to be comforting Eve as if to say *Be at peace now. My Son has righted the wrong done by you and Adam.*

...to Christ as the life-giving spring :
For with Thee is the fountain of life...

*...and to the Virgin Mary : **All creation rejoices in thee,
O thou who art full of grace** (Preveli Monastery, Crete)*

A composite icon of all the angels

The art
of icon painting...

...is still very much *alive*

CHAPTER

3.

A GUIDED TOUR

The Nave

The nave is full of symbolic objects and, while their location and exact form may vary from church to church, most of the following will be present.

CANDLES Near the door there is a desk or box containing candles. The first act of an Orthodox Christian on entering the church will be to take a candle (leaving a small donation in the collection box), light it and place it in the candle holder. The act of lighting a candle is, at its simplest level, a sort of "clocking on", the public statement that I have entered the House of God and am prepared for worship. However, the meaning of candles in the Orthodox Church is many faceted with deeper and deeper layers of symbolism.

The very early Christians, worshipping in the catacombs in secret and in fear of their lives, needed candles to see by and, in an era of electricity and light pollution, the candle is a reminder of those dark days. It is also a reminder that, although in the western world the main problem faced by Christians is indifference, persecution and suffering can still be their fate.

Candles, moreover, are a symbol of our devotion to God and respect for His saints. At weddings, baptisms, Easter and other festivals, they express spiritual joy, while at funerals, memorials and on Good Friday, they can express mourning and contrition. Many of you have probably seen the beautiful ceremony on Easter Saturday night when the candles of the faithful are lit from the "sacred flame" brought from Jerusalem and the joyful light of Christ's resurrection gradually spreads through the church and out into the streets. In contrast, there is a particularly moving moment during an Orthodox funeral service when the whole congregation, who have been holding lighted candles, blow them out simultaneously to symbolize the extinction of the earthly life and that the light of the loved one's life has departed. Finally, the wax of the candle, which becomes soft and pliable as it warms, symbolizes the tender heart ready to receive God's word, while the flame represents hearts that glow with the fire of God's love.

ICONS Also near the entrance to the church is an icon of the patron saint of the church. This icon is especially respected and is often surrounded with flowers or decorated with lace. Some churches, especially the larger churches in towns, also have a small stand, a little like a lectern, facing the door on which is placed a portable icon of the saint whose day it is. This not only honours the saint but enables people whose name day it is to pay their respects to their patron easily. Even the busiest of people can make time to pop into the church and kiss the icon of his or her saint. Another prominent icon will be that of the saint after whom the local bishop is named. Above some of the icons you will see a row of small metal disks and tokens hanging. These are symbolic offerings made to the saint when offering prayers for healing.

In churches with a dome, this is used to tremendous effect by creating a pictorial image of the "hier-archy of Heaven". First, the four evangelists are represented and above them the prophets and apostles. Higher still we see the archangels, John the Baptist and the virgin Mary and above all, in the centre of the dome, Christ the Almighty. The columns that support the roof of the nave depict other icons of the holy martyrs and doctors of the Church, the "pillars of Orthodoxy", while other saints and events from the Bible are painted on all the walls. Finally, on the western wall, the Last Judgement is often depicted, offering, as one leaves the church, a salutary warning on future behaviour!

THE PULPIT (Ambo) Some churches have a pulpit from which the sermon is preached and the Gospel read but this is not always the case. Many of the clergy prefer to preach the sermon standing on one of the lower steps of the sanctuary so that the impression is of a friend and guide or the father of a family rather than an instructor sending down messages from on high.

THE BISHOP'S THRONE Although the pulpit is optional, one item of furniture found in all Orthodox churches, however small, is the bishop's throne. This is usually placed in the nave towards the sanctuary, although it can be found inside the sanctuary behind the altar. If in the nave, it is always raised above ground level to symbolize the fact that, during worship, the bishop or archbishop represents Christ as pastor watching over his flock. Set into the back of the throne is an icon of Christ as the Great High Priest and Teacher, the roles in which the bishop represents Him. The elevation of the throne can present problems. A friend of mine recalls how, as a small altar boy, he was terrified of dropping the bishop's staff as he stretched up to hand it to him.

The Orthodox Church is, in the fullest sense, an "episcopal church", and the bishop is the central figure in its organisation. In general, he is much more "hands on" than his western equivalent, making a point of regularly visiting all the churches in his diocese and being readily available for anybody to visit him. He is the spiritual heir of the apostles and thus has a unique spiritual role as "ruler" of his diocese, as a teacher and interpreter of the faith and as celebrant of the Eucharist*. The Orthodox Church is hierarchical in its organization, with bishops, archbishops and pat-

---

* *Strictly speaking, when the priest preaches a sermon or celebrates the Eucharist, he is acting as the bishop's deputy.*

riarchs. However, in the spiritual sphere, all these ranks are equal as bishops. Of course, some posts such as that of Patriarch are treated with special respect but the Patriarch is strictly "first among equals". This was, in fact, one of the causes of the great split between the Orthodox east and the Roman Catholic west, the Great Schism of 1054. The former regarded (and still regards) the Pope as worthy of greater respect, as being the spiritual heir of St. Peter but nonetheless only the Bishop of Rome, while the latter regards him as supreme in spiritual matters*.

BOOKSTANDS To the right of the sanctuary steps is the bookstand, most larger churches having a second stand on the left. These contain the church service, hymn and prayer books. They are an important repository since the services in the Orthodox Church are extremely complex and need a library of about twenty large volumes. It is here that the readers and chanters stand during services.

CANDELABRAS and CHANDELIERS   On each

---

* The other major cause of the split was of great theological complexity and is outside the scope of this book. For a relatively clear explanation, see "The Orthodox Church" by Timothy Ware, which even I understood, almost!

side of the steps to the sanctuary, are large candle holders, while chandeliers are suspended from the ceiling of the nave. These represent the stars and the Heavenly light sent down from above and, although largely replaced by electrical fittings, they are still of a splendid beauty. At evening services, when all the lights are switched on at the entry of the priest, the dazzling glitter of the cut glass does give an impression of celestial brilliance.

SEATING As you look around the nave in various churches, you will usually see seating, ranging from a few chairs to rows of seats filling the nave. The general tradition and practise of the Orthodox Church was for churches to contain no seating at all. The effect thus created was of the family of God, clergy and laity, standing together to worship. This symbolism is most apparent during services where a bishop is present when much of the service takes place in the Nave with everybody standing together. "It is a remarkable thing how great a difference the presence or absence of pews can make to the whole spirit of Christian worship. There is in Orthodox worship a flexibility, an unselfconscious informality, not found among western congregations, at any rate north of the Alps. Western worshippers, ranged in their neat rows, all in their proper places, cannot move about during the service without causing a disturbance; a western congregation is generally expected to arrive at the beginning and to stay to the end. But in Orthodox worship people can come and go far more freely, and nobody is greatly surprised if they move about during the service"[1].

Candleholders

Bookstand   *Icon stand*

74

Pulpit

A modern saint, Nektarios, and the
symbolic offerings made to the saints

Bishop's throne

Chandelier:
Glory *to the* Thee **Who** has *shown* **forth** the light

*Although treated with the greatest respect,
the bishop is more father than ruler.
Here, Patriarch, bishop, clergy
and laity chat together informally*

The dome, *showing the* **hierarchly** *of* Heaven

The iconostasis

At the east end of the nave is a wooden or marble screen separating the nave from the sanctuary. This is the altar screen or Iconostasis. Usually ornately carved and richly decorated with icons, this represents the curtain dividing the tabernacle of the Old Testament into two parts - the Holy Place and the Holy of Holies. As mentioned above, I shall describe here the "classical" arrangement of icons on the more elaborate screens. However, this represents a strong tradition rather than any strict regulation and many variations can be found.

In the centre of the screen, there is a large door, called the Beautiful Gate on which is an icon of Christ as High Priest and King of Kings. This reminds us that, as High Priest he offered Himself as the ultimate sacrifice for our salvation. He is also the King of all and Head of the Church and so this door is also called the Royal Door. The Royal Door is only open during services and the Easter period and is only used by the priest when officiating and then only at certain prescribed times. Sometimes the priest uses the Royal Door to represent Christ coming into the world, for example, when the Gospel is read; at other moments he is representing the congregation and leads us symbolically into the presence of God. To the left and right of the central door are smaller doors leading to the sanctuary. These are used by the altar boys and the priest when not officiating.

To the right and left of the Royal Door are four icons. From left to right (facing) these are: the patron saint of the church, the Blessed Virgin Mary, Jesus Christ and St. John the Baptist. Many of the faithful, on entering the church, will pay respects to these icons in a particular order: first, Christ, as our Lord and Saviour, second Mary, as the Mother of Jesus, then St. John, the forerunner and baptiser of Jesus and finally the patron saint. Above each of these icons is hung an oil lamp which is kept burning at all times. These lamps represent our honour and respect to the saints, while the olive oil symbolizes the peace and mercy of God.

This pattern of icons is followed in all churches, of whatever size, although in the smaller chapels, the icon of St. John is occasionally omitted for reasons of space and the icon of the patron saint may be near the iconostasis rather than on it. Also often present are icons depicting the events in Christ's life cele-brated in the 12 great feasts of the Church. The remainder of the iconostasis is covered with other icons but there is no set arrangement or order. Many churches have an icon of the Last Supper above the Royal Door but this is by no means invariable.

In the larger churches with a double aisle, the layout is somewhat different. Here, the iconostasis is in two halves, one half serving each nave and each half having a central Royal Door. The right hand aisle is usually dedicated to the saint of the church and the right half of the iconostasis follows the normal arrangement of the four main icons. The left hand aisle is usually dedicated to another saint or aspect of God and the icons are related to that "theme".

The iconostasis

The Last Supper

Oil lamps honour the saints

The Royal Door

The Sanctuary

This is the area where the priest or bishop performs most of his duties during the services. Its predominant purpose is the celebration of the Divine Liturgy (Eucharist) and nearly everything present is related to this function.

THE ALTAR In the middle of the sanctuary is the altar, the holiest place in the church. This is where the consecration of the communion bread and wine takes place and represents Calvary, the Tomb and the Throne of Glory of Christ, all three being a single expression of Christ's sacrifice and triumph. It should be made of stone and contain some relics of the Holy Martyrs and Saints*. It is always covered with three cloths, usually white, representing the coverings in which the dead body of Christ was shrouded and in which He was buried, and symboliz-

---

* *"Because Orthodox are convinced that the body is sanctified and transfigured together with the soul, they have an immense reverence for the relics of the saints. Like Roman Catholics, they believe that the grace of God present in the saints' bodies during life remains active in their relics when they have died and that God uses these relics as a channel of divine power and instrument of healing"*[2].

ing the purity of thought which should be brought to the Communion service.

Several items are kept permanently on the altar when not in use.

THE HOLY GOSPEL The Holy Gospel, with gold or silver covers, is richly ornamented with engraved icons, the Resurrection on the front and the Crucifixion on the back. On the corners are representations of the four Evangelists, Matthew, Mark, Luke and John. The Gospel rests on a silk cloth illustrated with the burial of Christ. This cloth, the Eliton, is spread on the altar during the Eucharist. Since the Gospel contains the words of God through Jesus, this book is treated with great respect and reverence. During the Communion Service and in some other services, it is carried out of the Sanctuary by the priest, symbolizing the coming of Christ into the world. **IMPORTANT NOTE:** The Gospel, and indeed other items on the altar, are of great beauty and it may be tempting to approach close to the Sanctuary to examine them more closely. Please do not. Many Gospels and other church items are on display in museums, especially those attached to monasteries and cathedrals, where you can examine them at your leisure without the risk of offending.

THE TABERNACLE Also called the Receptacle of the Holy Gifts, this is of gold or silver and is in the shape of a sepulchre. This is used to store the consecrated bread and wine for the sick in an emergency and at certain times during Lent when the consecration does not take place during the Liturgy. However, the Blessed Sacrament is only reserved for these purposes and there is no equivalent to the Roman Catholic services of Exposition and Benediction.

THE CROSS This small, hand-held cross is used by the priest to bless the worshippers during the Liturgy.

CANDLESTICKS 2 or 4 candles which are lit during the Liturgy and represent Christ "the true Light".

Behind the altar can be seen the following:

HOLY CROSS and EXAPTERYGA A beautiful silver cross fixed to a pole stands between 2 circular banners, also on poles. These banners are called Exapteryga ("Six Wings") and are engraved with images of the six-winged angels called Seraphim who guard the throne of God. The Cross and Exapteryga are carried in procession on important feast days and stand in the nave during Holy Week.

CRUCIFIX A large wooden cross on which a life-sized representation of the body of Christ is fixed on the Thursday before Easter and removed on Good Friday. This is usually placed in a conspicuous position to remind worshippers of the sacrifice of Christ. During the Easter period it can be seen in the nave.

To the left of the altar, not usually visible from the nave is the CHAPEL OF THE PREPARATION (Prothesis). In this is a table, cupboard or space in the wall where the accessories used in the preparation of the Eucharist are kept. It is also used to store the bread and wine offered by the members of the congregation for the Liturgy. It is the custom for these to be supplied by the faithful, usually given to the priest at Vespers the evening before the Liturgy. Any member of the church can make these offerings but people make a point of supplying the gifts on special occasions such as name days.

To the right of the altar is the DIAKONIKON, generally used as a vestry, where other items used in the services are kept. These include the lanterns, torches or candles held by the altar boys in procession and the censer for burning incense. The CENSER is usually made of silver and hangs from three chains with small bells. The use of incense is of great antiquity dating back to the time of Moses. When censing the altar and the icons, the priest is showing honour to Christ and His saints. The censing of the worshippers represents our prayers ascending to Heaven.

ICONS Within the sanctuary, there are paintings of the Church Fathers, authors of liturgies and other sanctified priests and deacons so that the priest, as it were, celebrates the Eucharist in the presence of his predecessors. Above, the Eucharist itself is represented by the communion of the apostles, the sharing of bread on the left and of wine on the right. Above these and directly behind the altar is the Virgin Mary in her role as intercessor for mankind with the image of Christ above her. Finally, at the top of the vault a representation of Pentecost indicates the permanent presence of the Holy Spirit.

The altar

Benediction crosses

The Tabernacle

The Holy Gospel

"For Thou art the Source of light for our souls and bodies"

*Relics of the saints, usually a small piece
of bone set in wax for protection*

*Holy Cross and Exapteryga, seraphim
guarding the throne of God*

The crucifix, empty in preparation for Easter

Icons in the sanctuary

WORSHIP

General

To the best of my knowledge, visitors are welcome to attend services in the Orthodox Church. In fact, in my own church in a village very popular with tourists, the local priests have included some prayers in English and Latin for the benefit of visitors. Many people use the occasion for their own quiet prayers and meditation in an atmosphere of extreme beauty, others are curious about what goes on. Whatever your reasons for attending, the following notes may help.

BEHAVIOUR Although the locals are often surprisingly informal in their dress and you are not

expected to be in your "Sunday Best", anyone entering the church is expected to be dressed soberly. Secondly, as mentioned below, the worshippers often
display a lack of formality and "stuffiness" but I suggest that visitors show a reasonable degree of respect
while in church. The rule is basically: "Behave as you
feel you should in church, not necessarily as the locals do". I have actually seen someone answer a mobile phone during a service but after the bolt of light-
ning that shot from the eye of the officiating priest, I
don't think it will happen again for quite some time!

A GLIMPSE OF HEAVEN As you sit or stand
surrounded by the beauty of the icons, the air filled
with incense, watching the priests in their magnifi-
cent robes and listening to the ancient tones of the
plainchant, you may feel that, for a moment, you are
outside the normal bustle of everyday life. In this you
have, without knowing it, captured a basic theological
truth of Orthodox worship: that the services are a
meeting point between earth and Heaven, a moment
when time and eternity touch. Thus, the icons of the
saints become crucial in uniting the living, earthly
members of the Church with the "angels and archangels and all the host of Heaven"[3]. "The faithful can

feel that the walls of the church open out upon eternity, and they are helped to realize that their liturgy on earth is one and the same with the great Liturgy of heaven"[4]. Of course, there is much more to the meaning of the various services but it is this theme that underpins everything else.

INFORMALITY At the same time, there is a surprising air of "reverent informality" in Orthodox worship. The reverence is always present and yet people generally feel "at home". We are in God's house, certainly, but it is the house of our Father and Friend. This paradox is almost impossible to describe if you have not experienced it but a few examples from my own observation may help. An old woman makes a deep obeisance before the icon of the Virgin Mary on the iconostasis and notices a spot of oil on the floor, so she gets out her handkerchief and wipes it up. A priest has problems blowing out a candle during the Easter morning service and both priest and altar boy have great difficulty keeping straight faces.

My wife and I were baptized into the Orthodox Church as adults and, not having been brought up in the Church and speaking little Greek, we were very nervous. Although the service was very solemn and moving, the priests were continually asking us if we were alright and trying to put us at our ease. Finally, I don't think I have ever been in a church where Christ's command to "let the little children come to me" is taken so literally. Although children are taught from a very early age not to go up the sanctuary steps, they are allowed to wander fairly freely in the church and nobody worries. When giving communion to children, the priest will chat to them or try to comfort the babies if they cry.

SEATING As mentioned above, the general absence of seating enables more freedom of movement among the worshippers and, in long services, people will take it in turns to sit. If you attend a service, feel free to use the seats but also be conscious of the needs of others especially the old and infirm. It is also the custom in most Greek churches for the men to stand or sit on the right and the women on the left. Another advantage of this flexibility of movement is that the congregation, especially on major feast days, can often be much bigger than the church can hold. Thus, although some of the congregation stay inside for the whole service, it is the custom for most to enter the church, pay obeisance to the icon, stay for a while and then leave to stand outside, allowing others to enter.

On more normal occasions, although many people stand for the whole service, it is permitted to sit during the hymns, many of the prayers, readings other than the Gospel and during the sermon. There is no strict rule about when to stand and the best guide is to sit somewhere near the back and follow the general consensus. The congregation always stands at the beginning of the service when the bells ring, for processions of the clergy through the nave, during the reading of the Gospel, at the consecration of the Communion bread and wine and when the priest blesses or censes the congregation.

THE SIGN OF THE CROSS Flexibility also exists with regard to when people make the sign of the cross. Orthodox vary considerably in the frequency with which they cross themselves during services, some doing it almost continuously, others occasionally. However, most people cross themselves on entering the church, when the priest blesses or censes them and when the Holy Trinity is mentioned in prayers. Outside the church, many cross themselves before a meal and when passing a church. This latter custom has been described to me rather charmingly by a theologian as "saying good morning to the Lord". In the Orthodox Church, the sign is made with the thumb and first two fingers of the right hand and from right to left. Roman Catholics and Anglicans, on the other hand, use only the thumb and forefinger and cross from left to right. The latter usage is, in fact, older but there are strong theological arguments to justify both methods*. Nevertheless, the essential purpose and meaning of this ancient sign remain the same. Making the sign of the cross represents both an acknowledgement of God in our hearts and minds and public proclamation that we are Christians. It is often used also as a brief, wordless prayer.

LANGUAGE It has always been the practice of the Orthodox Church to use the local language for its services. The two exceptions are Greece, where they have retained Byzantine Greek, and Russia, where

---

* The two fingers and thumb held close together symbolize the Holy Trinity, the three persons of God having a single will, substance and spiritual energy. The forehead represents God in Heaven who sent Christ down to earth (the stomach) for our salvation. Christ ascended to Heaven and sits on the right hand of God (right shoulder) from where he will judge us, setting the righteous on the right and the unrepentant on the left (Hell).

they continue to use Old Slavonic. So don't worry if you don't understand the words as many of the congregation are not too sure either! Just as in the days when Roman Catholic services were in Latin, the faithful have a good idea of the general drift but not always the detail*. Although there is some debate about updating the language, the use of traditional Greek has the advantage of continuity and avoids the problems of modern language needing to be continually modernized further, resulting in the confusion reigning in the Anglican Church.

MUSIC All services in the Orthodox Church are chanted and, in Greece, the Byzantine style of plainchant is used. Although not forbidden, there is no tradition in Orthodoxy for music other than plainchant to be used in services. Having been brought up an Anglican, I do sometimes miss singing my old favourite hymns and the western churches have undoubtedly been enriched by the talents of the great composers. However, the simplicity and beauty of

---

* Those Catholics who remember the Latin Mass will at least understand one of the more frequent responses - Kyrie Eleison (Lord have mercy) - as this very ancient prayer was included in their service in the original Greek.

the plainchant certainly helps to create that sense of "differentness", of a world outside time that is such a feature of Orthodox worship. Alexis, Patriarch of Moscow, put the case succinctly, if a touch forcefully, in 1945. "To sing liturgical hymns in the shrill manner of worldly songs or of the passionate tunes of opera is to deprive the faithful of any possibility of concentrating, as well as of grasping the contents and the meaning of the hymns"[5]. And he was talking about Victorian ballads and composers like Verdi and Schubert. I wonder what he would have made of Cliff Richard or Folk Masses*.

All the hymns, responses and some of the prayers are sung by the chanters. These are not exactly a choir in the western sense (in a small village church there is often only one) but represent the congregation in the services. This is not so much a matter of theology as of tradition and convenience. As mentioned above, the services of the Orthodox Church are complex,

---

* This tradition does not apply to the use of secular music outside the services. In recent years, a group of "Rocking Monks" have topped the charts in Greece with pop music on a religious theme. Although some of the more conservative clergy have been outraged, the general opinion of the Church has been supportive.

with very many variations so that a great deal of training and experience is needed to "get it right". Even for
the chanters, especially during the many services of
Easter, confusion can set in, requiring a discreet helping hand from the priest to point them in the right
direction. The chanters are by tradition always men,
although on Good Friday the service contains a beautiful hymn when a woman's choir sings alternate
verses. Congregational singing is unusual at present
in services in Greece, although it is certainly not
forbidden and many of the older members of the
congregation will often join in some of the better
known hymns. However, the predominant use of
trained chanters does ensure that the beauty of the
Byzantine plainchant is preserved more or less intact.
(Although, it is true that the quality of the chanting
does vary considerably, especially in small villages).

The Communion bread...

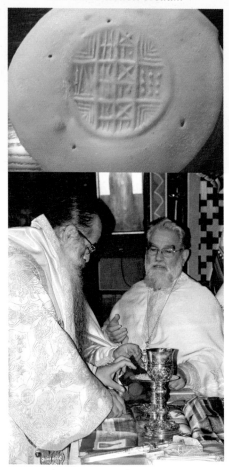

...and preparation for Communion

The Word of God

Clergy and laity join the Liturgy on earth...

...with the great Liturgy of Heaven
"Now the powers of Heaven with us, invisibly worship."
(Church of St. Catherine, Iraklion, Crete)

Priests

There are two types of priest ("Papas" in Greek) in the Orthodox Church, celibate and married. Since a priest may not marry after ordination, he must decide before ordination to which order he wishes (or is called) to belong and this decision is irreversible. Generally, the married clergy become parish priests and, as family men, are better suited to the pastoral side of the priesthood. The celibate clergy are monastic and it is from this group that bishops and other officials of the Church are selected. Thus, the Orthodox Church seems to have made irrelevant the argument in the Western Church between those who believe the clergy can and should be married in order to better understand and care for their flock and those who believe the clergy should remain without worldly commitments in order to devote their time fully to God and the Church*.

The most noticeable thing about Orthodox priests,

---

* *The Orthodox Church is unanimous in its rejection of the possibility of the ordination of women to the priesthood. However, there is a long tradition of deaconesses and, although the practice of ordaining women to the diaconate has largely died out, there is a lot of support for its revival.*

whatever their calling, is their strikingly patriarchal air resulting from their long hair and beards. In my early visits to Greece, I sometimes wondered irreverently if a bald man could become a priest! I found out later that the simple answer is "Yes". According to Christian belief, Man is made in the image of God and therefore, whatever has been given to us should not be tinkered with for reasons of personal vanity or fashion. In the early Church, it was therefore the practice of all Christians to leave their hair and beards untrimmed and, although the custom died out for the laity, it is still the general practice, though not a strict rule, for the clergy. Recently, there have been requests by some younger priests to get rid of the long beards, black robes and pipe hats and adopt a more modern look but these have been firmly rejected by the Church authorities.

*The long hair of the priests, as well as the vestments,
all have theological significance*

Regular Services

The main services of the Orthodox Church follow broadly the same pattern as other Christian denominations namely an evening service (Esperinos), roughly equivalent to Vespers, a morning service (Orthros) like Matins and the Holy Communion or Divine Liturgy. Timing and frequency vary considerably according to the time of year and location but generally in the main churches there is an evening and morning service on most days, with Matins on Sunday morning followed immediately by Holy Communion. If your only experience of Orthodox worship is the great feast days, you may feel that the services are of inordinate length compared with the western churches. However, on ordinary days, the morning and evening services last less than an hour and Holy Communion takes from one and a quarter to one and a half hours, depending on the length of the sermon. Remember, of course, that it is not necessary to stay for the whole service.

You can also take comfort from the fact that the Russian Orthodox services are, on the whole, even longer. Paul of Aleppo, a 17th century Arab Orthodox travelling in Russia, wrote in his diary, "And now we enter on our travail and anguish. For all their churches are empty of seats. There is not one, even, for the bishop; you see the people all through the service standing like rocks, motionless or incessantly bending with their devotions. God help us for the length of their prayers and chants and Masses, for we suffered great pain, so that our very souls were tortured with fatigue and anguish... As for the Muscovites, their feet must surely be of iron"6. I think this must apply to some of the old ladies in our local church.

HOLY COMMUNION Orthodox generally do not take Holy Communion every Sunday and, in fact, will usually only take it if they feel completely prepared and in the right frame of mind. Usually, though not invariably, they will have been to confession before-hand and completely fast on the morning before the service*. Confession is not as formal as in the Roman Catholic Church and usually takes place with priest and penitent standing near the iconostasis. The Com-

---

* To my consternation, I found that the fast includes coffee and cigarettes! However, when I realized that the priest gets up at 5 and has to wait for his coffee and a cigarette until after Communion at 9.30, I decided that an hour's abstinence wasn't too much to ask.

munion bread, following the oldest traditions of the Church, is normal leavened bread. During the consecration, the bread is broken up and placed in the chalice with the wine. When giving Communion the priest takes a piece of bread and a little wine on a spoon and gives it to the receiver. Although not everyone takes Communion, after the final blessing, all the congregation receive a piece of bread, called "αntidoron", which has been blessed but not consecrated. Generally, non-Orthodox present at the service are allowed and encouraged to share in this as an expression of Christian fellowship and love.

Outdoor services *are* popular throughout *Greece*

FEΛSTS

The Calendar

Before looking at some of the important Feast Days and celebrations you may come across in Greece, it might be useful to mention the calendar. I usually manage to confuse people utterly when I try to explain why the Orthodox Easter is different from the Western Church and why some countries have Christmas on 6th January but here goes.

The Julian Calendar, devised by the Romans, was used throughout Europe until the 16th century. However, in 1582, Pope Gregory XIII authorized a revision, resulting in the New (Gregorian) Calendar. This resulted in dates shifting 13 days forward, January 1st, for example, becoming January 13th. The new calendar was immediately adopted in all Roman Catholic countries and the Protestant countries in western Europe followed gradually, in spite of riots demanding the return of the 13 days lost! This is the calendar with which we are all familiar.

In the Orthodox world, however, the Julian Calendar continued to be used until 1924 when it was revised to correspond to the New Calendar. Although most governments accepted the change, because the revision was not a matter of faith or dogma and was not the result of a general council of the Church, it was only accepted in some churches, including Greece* and Cyprus, while others such as Russia continued to use the Old Calendar. Thus, all religious festivals in Russia and Serbia fall 13 days after those in countries using the Gregorian Calendar**. To

---

* *The monastic communities on Mount Athos, which is semi-autonomous from Greece, maintain the Julian Calendar. There are also, in Greece itself, a small minority of monasteries and parishes which adhere to the Old Calendar, although their influence is now very small.*

** *This calendar change is also why, during the Soviet era, the 1917 October Revolution was actually commemorated in November.*

complicate matters still further, the date of Easter is still set in all Orthodox countries including Greece according to the Julian Calendar so that it is usually between one and five weeks later than the western date, the two corresponding about every four years.

Although not directly related to the theme of this book, while on the subject of dates, you might find, as I did, that you do a "double take" when you see a war memorial. Instead of the familiar "1914-18, 1939-45" you will see "1912-22, 1940-49". This is because Greece was involved in the Balkan Wars which immediately preceded the First World War and continued the war with Turkey after 1918. She joined the Second World War when Italy invaded in 1940 and a civil war followed on from the liberation in 1945.

Easter

Although Christmas is a very important festival in the Orthodox church, Easter is the "Feast of Feasts". After all, while the birth of the Saviour is an event worthy of celebration, birth is shared by all humanity. Only Christ, however, rose from the dead and so the Resurrection must be viewed as the culmination of God's purpose*. The name given to the feast in Greek is "Pascha" which is the Greek word for Passover, the Jewish feast. This reminds us not only that Christ's death and resurrection occurred during the Passover period but also of the continuity between the Jewish tradition and Christianity and the fact that, just as the Passover represented God's first covenant with the Jews, so Easter represents God's second covenant with all mankind.

If you are fortunate enough to be in Greece during the Easter period, you have the opportunity to participate in a unique and powerful experience. The week before Easter (Holy Week) is called in the Orthodox Church "Great Week" (Megali Evdomada) and each day is called "Great", for example, "Great Monday" etc. There are morning and evening services throughout the week, but it is outside the scope of this book to describe the events in detail. The following is a list of those services likely to be of interest to the casual visitor. You may be a little confused because everything seems to happen a day early. For example, the crucifixion is commemorated

* *For, if the dead rise not, then is not Christ raised; and if Christ be not raised, your faith is vain. 1 Cor. 15; 16-17*

on the Thursday night. This is because the Orthodox Church follows Biblical tradition in starting the day at sunset.

PALM SUNDAY On the Sunday before Easter, Christ's entry into Jerusalem is commemorated in the morning Liturgy and crosses made of palm leaves are distributed at the end of the service. The church is often decorated with olive branches and people break off a few leaves to keep with the palm.

GREAT THURSDAY In the evening, a beautiful service takes place during which the Holy Cross with the effigy of Christ is decorated with wreaths and flowers. During the night, the bier is prepared by members of the church and adorned with flowers. This is another illustration of the reverent informality of the Orthodox Church as, in spite of the solemnity of the ceremony, one of my Greek friend's happiest memories is playing "Hide and Seek" around the church as a child while her mother helped with the decoration.

GREAT FRIDAY (Good Friday) A solemn service in the evening at which hymns of lamentation are sung by choirs of men and women culminates in the funeral procession of the crucified Christ. The decorated bier, on which lies an icon of Christ, is carried in solemn procession through the town or village. Candles and lanterns line the streets and lights in the houses, shops and bars are turned off as the cortege passes. At certain points along the route, the procession stops and prayers are said for anyone in the area who is sick or who has died during the previous year. In some areas, people throw flowers from the balconies onto the bier. This must be one of the most moving and beautiful ceremonies in any Christian denomination.

GREAT SATURDAY The culmination of Easter Week is the Great Matins service beginning at about 11pm on Easter Saturday. As the time approaches midnight, all the lights are extinguished apart from a single candle that has been lit from the holy flame in the Church of the Resurrection in Jerusalem. The priest lights his candle from the flame and, in turn, lights the candles of other priests and deacons. Gradually the rest of the congregation light their candles and the light of Christ's resurrection spreads through the church and out into the street where the congregation who could not get into church are waiting. All, including non-Orthodox, are welcome to join in the lighting of candles. Traditionally, godparents give their godchildren beautifully decorated candles to light at Easter but the commercialism of Christmas which we bemoan in the western Church has hit Easter in Greece and "Barbie Doll" and "Power Rangers" candles are all too popular!

The priests and congregation now leave the church, representing the disciples coming to the garden on the morning of the resurrection. The service outside also has the practical benefit that everybody can join in the supreme moment of resurrection. More prayers are said and hymns are sung until, at exactly midnight, the priest chants the words "Christos Anesti" (Christ is risen). At this point all hell breaks out (if that is not an inappropriate phrase!). The bells ring, firecrackers explode, boats sound their sirens, guns are fired in the air (illegal but still common in the villages), in some places even dynamite is thrown into lakes or gorges. The whole of Greece seems to want to make as much noise as possible to celebrate the resurrection of the Saviour*. Also at midnight an effigy of Judas is burnt. Although

---

* *Unfortunately, in most places in Greece, people don't*

this has no basis in theology and is frowned on by the church., it is a social tradition of great antiquity in Greece.

After the celebrations, most people go home to break their fast with a traditional meal of soup and lamb but, for the devout, there is a Communion Service back in the church. The solemn re-entry into the church represents the entry of the disciples into the tomb to find it empty and Christ risen. The lit candles are carried home (in windy conditions keeping them alight can be a major challenge) and, with the smoke, the sign of the cross is made on the front door before entering. After midnight and for at least the following week, you will hear Orthodox greet each other with the words "Christos Anesti" instead of "kalimera". The response is "Alithos Anesti" (He is risen indeed). The other greeting is common to all feast days, holidays, birthdays or name days : "Chronia Polla" (Many Years).

wait for midnight to set off the fireworks and the solemnity and beauty of the service is all too often spoiled by the continuous and premature bangs of firecrackers. If you are looking for a quieter, more spiritual experience, I suggest attending the service at one of the convents or monasteries.

EASTER SUNDAY Because of the late celebrations of Easter Saturday, the services on Easter Sunday morning are usually somewhat quieter affairs, although I am still surprised at the number who actually make it. The "Service of Love" is full of joy and the hymns are some of the most beautiful in the Orthodox tradition. Much of the service takes place in the nave, giving a greater sense of the Church as a family and the entire congregation join in the hymn "Christos Anesti". (In many churches, the Gospel of the day is read in several languages to symbolize God's message of love reaching out to everyone in the world regardless of nationality).

The bier prepared for Good Friday
(right p.) The Crucifixion

The Good Friday funeral procession
(right p.) The Resurrection

The Great Matins of Easter Saturday

*No, it's not Guy Fawkes but Judas Iscariot
ready for his yearly comeuppance*

Other Feast Days

To list all the other feasts of the Church is impossible in this brief guide but I will mention a few that may be of interest to visitors. I have restricted myself mainly to religious festivals although there are, of course, many other celebrations and local traditions throughout Greece, which you will probably find described in local guide books. It is worth noting here that the Orthodox Church is the established church in Greece and thus even secular occasions always have a religious element. Western Church equivalents are shown in brackets where appropriate.

Public holidays in Greece are always on the date of the holiday, even if they fall at weekends, so it is a matter of luck whether we actually get an extra day off or not.

ASCENSION DAY (40 days after Easter). Very often the service is held in a church high up in the mountains, which makes this a beautiful open air experience on a pleasant May or June morning.

PENTECOST (50 days after Easter) (Whitsunday). A public holiday, called Trinity Day in Greece to emphasize the importance of the Holy Spirit as part of the Trinity

TRANSFIGURATION OF CHRIST (6th August). At the service on this day, the fruits of the field are blessed, similar to the Harvest Festival in the western Church.

DORMITION (Falling Asleep) of the Mother of God *(15th August).* Equivalent to the Roman Catholic Assumption Day, this is a public holiday and a major feast day, not only because of the reverence paid to the Virgin Mary by Orthodox but because it is the name day of Maria's, of whom there are a vast number in Greece. It is the opportunity for family gatherings and parties all over Greece and travel is definitely not recommended between the 14th and 16th August! 15th August is also the memorial day for the Greek destroyer "Elli", blown up with all hands by an Italian submarine on Assumption Day 1940. This act led shortly afterwards to Greece's entry into the war.

"OCHI DAY" (28th October) This is not strictly a religious festival, being the anniversary of the declaration of war with Italy in 1940. The Italian government had offered Greece an impossible ultimatum to which

the leader Metaxas responded with the simple word "Ochi" (No). However, religious services play a very important part in this Greek equivalent of Remembrance Day. In all towns and villages, a service of remembrance takes place at the war memorial, one minute's silence is observed and wreathes are laid. This is particularly moving because of the involvement of the children as well as the military and civic dignitaries. To watch two kindergarten infants toddle to the memorial holding a wreath bigger than they are will bring a lump to the throat of the hardest hearted onlooker.

Entry of the MOTHER of GOD into the TEMPLE (21st November). Celebrating the consecration of Mary to the service of God at the age of 3, this feast day has particular significance in Crete where it is celebrated by many as the name day of unmarried girls called Maria.

NATIVITY of CHRIST (25th December) (Christmas). As mentioned above, Christmas is less of a celebration than Easter and is largely a religious holiday and family affair. However, the influence of television has led to the children expecting (and getting) presents at Christmas as well as Easter.

ST. VASILI (1st January). The 1st of January, besides being New Year's Day, is also the feast of the Circumcision of Christ and the commemoration of St. Basil the Great (St. Vasilios), one of the Fathers of the Church. Although not directly related to the religious festival, in many parts of Greece there is a delightful (relatively modern) custom whereby St. Vasili, dressed remarkably like Santa Claus, visits and distributes presents to the children. So, in answer to my grandchildren's worried question when I first moved to Greece: yes, Father Christmas does visit Greece; he just has a different name and calls a little later!

THEOPHANIA (6th January) (Epiphany). This commemorates the baptism of Christ and outside services are held to bless the waters, mostly the sea and rivers but, at inland locations, lakes or even reservoirs are used. At the end of the service the priest throws a cross into the water and young people dive in to retrieve it. The person who retrieves the cross receives a replica and a blessing for the year. Although the divers have traditionally been young men, in the last couple of years a few girls have joined in successfully in some places

During the weeks after Theophania, the priest visits houses and businesses throughout the parish to hold a brief service of blessing. If you are here in January and suddenly find yourself in the middle of a blessing when you go to buy your bread, don't worry. Just stand quietly until the end and accept the blessing as covering the customers as well as the staff.

THE THREE HIERARCHS (30th January). The feast day of three of the most important early Church Fathers, Basil the Great, Gregory the Theologian and John Chrysostom. It is a popular feast day with children and teachers as it is a school holiday.

"CLEAN MONDAY" (40 days before Easter). Roughly equivalent to Ash Wednesday, the first day of Lent, this is the beginning of the great fast before Easter and, this being Greece, is the opportunity for a party! Being a public holiday, the tradition is that families go out into the countryside for a picnic where, although the food is suitable for the fast, (see next section) there is plenty of it and deliciously cooked. It is also traditional to fly kites on this day which has theological significance as representing the flight of the soul towards Heaven but, for most people, is simply fun for "children" of all ages.

ANNUNCIATION (25th March) (Lady Day). The celebration of the Archangel Gabriel's annunciation to the Virgin Mary that she would bear the son of God is a public holiday of both religious and secular importance. On Annunciation Day 1821, Bishop Germanos of Patras raised the flag of revolt against the Ottoman Turkish rulers. Because independence came to different parts of Greece at different times*, there is no single "Independence Day" so it is the beginning of the revolt that is celebrated as Greek National Day. Services are held throughout the country and, as with Ochi Day, the children play an important part, reciting poems about the struggle for freedom.

CHURCH NAME DAYS (Various dates) A special celebration is held in each church on the feast day of its patron. In villages, the name day of the main church becomes a great village feast with the evening service followed by a procession of the icon of the saint concerned. This is usually followed by a party with dancing and fireworks, often lasting into the early hours of the morning.

OTHER MAJOR FESTIVALS Nativity of the Mother of God *(8 September)* Exaltation of the Cross *(14 September)*.

---

* *The Dodecanese Islands did not become part of the Greek State until 1948!*

The Dormition of the Mother of God

the **whole** *community*
participates in
Ochi **Day**
and National **Day**
including *children*
(*and the* war **widows**!)

Young men dive for the cross at Theophania

The Nativity of Christ

Yes, "Santa Claus" does visit Greece

St. Vasili meets the bishop

CHAPTER

6.

FΛSTS

While the Greeks certainly enjoy their religious festivals and feast days, they also take the observation of fasts surprisingly seriously*. Having been brought up merely not to eat meat on Good Friday and to give up chocolate for

---

* *As mentioned previously, Orthodox believe in the potential holiness of the whole person, body as well as soul. Thus fasting plays two essential roles. First, it is a process of training and disciplining the body so that bodily needs do not entirely dominate our lives. Secondly, it is intentionally harsh: in an age when martyrdom for the faith is rare and especially in a country where to be a Christian is easy, fasting is a reminder that the way of the Christian can involve sacrifice.*

Lent, the rigour of the Orthodox fasts caused me some culture shock. For the 40 days of Lent, not only is meat given up but all dairy products as well and, in Holy week, a strict fast, even oil is abandoned and we are basically restricted to salads and boiled vegetables. Although outside the monasteries and clergy, not everyone follows the fast for the whole period of Lent, many people including youngsters do observe it and the vast majority of Orthodox follow the full fast for Holy Week. So, if you notice a slight short-ness of temper among some of the locals just before Easter, remember they might be very, very hungry!

For the devout, moreover, fasting is not confined to Lent. The 40 days before Christmas, the 14 days before 15th August, a period of between 1 and 6 weeks before the Feast of Ss. Peter and Paul on 29th June, various other days and every Wednesday and Friday are fasts of varying degrees of rigour. The period before Christmas, for example, is a "Happy Fast" and fish is allowed until the 12th December. Having said all that, the Orthodox Church is not totally prescriptive about the rules and leaves the extent and frequency of fasts largely up to one's own conscience. While encouraging fasting as a discipline of the body and an act of self-sacrifice, it recognizes that this is essentially a matter between the individual and God.

The value of fasting may not be entirely spiritual. The traditional health and longevity of the Greeks, in spite of their high cigarette consumption, has long been attributed to the healthy "Mediterranean diet" but frequent fasting may well have played an important role. The Orthodox Church seems to have invented the "Detox diet" some 1500 years before the Californians! Unfortunately, the declining frequency of fasting coupled with the increasing consumption of junk food is rapidly changing the statistics. However, the Greeks have remained remarkably ingenious in devising interesting dishes from very restricted ingredients and if you are a vegetarian or vegan, you will still find a wide range of tasty dishes in the more traditional tavernas especially during fast periods. Ask for food which is "nistisimos", i.e. suitable for fasts*.

For those of you who are partial to escargots, snails are exempt from the fast and, especially in Crete are a great delicacy. Personally. I'd rather stick to the boiled vegetables.

A **new** *meaning to* **Fast Food**:
Greek **cuisine** *offers an*
extraordinary **variety** *of tasty dishes for* Lent.

CHAPTER

7.

FAMILY OCCASIONS

Greece is a country to which many people return year after year and the Greeks are deservedly famous for their hospitality and friendliness. Therefore, visitors may well be invited to join in the celebrations of family life and these notes may help.

Baptisms

Nearly all Greek children are baptized into the Church at an early age although adult baptism is becoming more common as more immigrants join the Orthodox Church. The Orthodox, like the Anglicans and Roman Catholics, believe in child baptism because they follow literally the words of Christ "Let the little children come to me". However, they go one step further in accepting the child into full participation in the Church, including the taking of Holy Communion. Thus, there is no confirmation service at a later age. They believe that neither God's love nor membership of the Church should have preconditions, such as the ability to exercise choice or rational thought. The entirety of God's grace is available to all, adult and baby alike.

Baptism is by total immersion, although for practical reasons adults are baptized by the water being poured over their heads and bodies (in seemingly enormous quantities in my case). The godmother ("nona") or godfather ("nonos"), only one godparent being required, play a very important role in the baptism, actually helping to anoint the baby with the holy oil. They take their duties extremely seriously and, in Greece, the relationship between godparent and godchild is often as strong as between parent and child and lasts for life. It is the godparent who provides the cross worn by the newly baptized and the white "robe of light" put on the child after baptism, not to mention a complete new "Sunday best" outfit for after the service.

After the actual baptism, two further rites take place. First the child is anointed with a special oil, blessed by the bishop and called "chrism". While the baptism represents the spiritual death and resurrection of the candidate, the chrism represents the coming of the Holy Spirit into his or her life. Finally, a symbolic lock of hair is cut off to represent the candidate's first act of sacrifice to God. Then the congregation wish the child and godparent "Na Zisetai" (roughly, "Live long") and it is time for the party.

Name Days

In Greece, babies are usually named after grandparents; for example, the first son will be called after his father's father the second after his mother's father. This is a social tradition and has no particular religious significance. The Church, however, does insist that babies are only christened with the name of a saint. Thus, on joining the Orthodox Church, my wife chose to be baptized as "Eleni" since her existing name was not a saint. I was lucky as "Christopher" merely had to be changed to the Greek version - "Christophoros".

Because of this, the feast day of the saint after

whom you are named becomes a very important celebration. One's "Name Day" is still often regarded as more important than one's birthday, although the children seem to be gradually converting relations to the idea of presents on their birthday as well as their name day. Certainly, in rural areas until the not too distant past, people were often not sure of the date of their birthday whereas the name day was certain. If you are aware that it is a Greek friend's name day, the traditional greeting of "Chronia Polla" will be appreciated. The saints' days of the most common Greek names are listed in Appendix 3.

Baptismal font

A priest blessing the water. The grace of God is freely availlable to all...

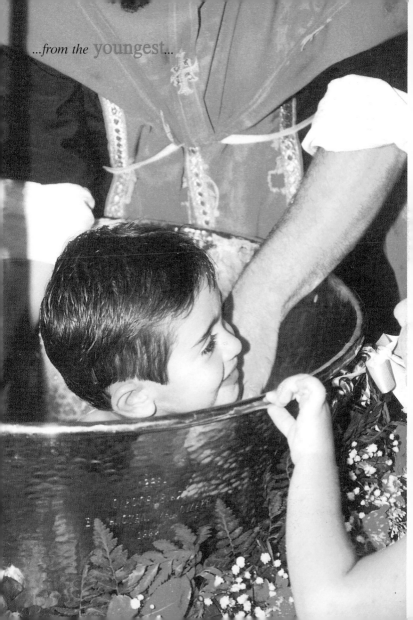

...from the youngest...

to the slightly **older**
(the author receiving baptism)

Weddings

The wedding service in the Orthodox Church is, strictly speaking, two separate services although the second now follows immediately after the first. The blessing and exchange of rings is, in fact, the service of betrothal and represents the promise of the couple to live together as man and wife*. The beautiful ceremony of crowning is the actual sacrament of marriage and is full of symbolism. The crowns are, in Greece, usually circlets of artificial pearls of varying elaborateness (and expense) joined together with a white ribbon. They are, first and foremost, the outward sign of God's blessing on the marriage and a prefiguring of the crown of glory we will receive in Heaven. They are also crowns of joy as the "king and queen" of a new family "kingdom" are crowned. Finally, and surprisingly on such a happy occasion, they represent crowns of martyrdom, not

---

* *The Orthodox Church in Cyprus some years ago decided to reinstate the traditional separation of the betrothal and marriage service. However, too many couples took the betrothal as the Church's blessing on them living together with obvious results. Reluctantly, and perhaps sadly, the Church in Cyprus has now returned to the more modern procedure.*

in a negative sense but because a truly happy marriage always involves an element of self-sacrifice on both sides. After the priest has crowned the couple, the best man or woman (Koumbaros or Koumbara) exchange the crowns three times between the bride and groom. He or she (only one is necessary) actually has a religious role in the wedding service, introducing the couple into the church. Often, he or she will later be the godparent of the couple's first child.

The most striking difference between an Orthodox wedding and its western counterpart is that the bride and groom do not say a word. In some versions of the service, they recite the Lord's Prayer but there is no exchange of vows*. This is because the promise to stay together as man and wife is implicit in the wish to be married. The sacrament of marriage represents the blessing of God and the Church on this wish. The fact that there is no "contractual" oath does not lessen

---

*There is, however, a recent social custom which, though strongly disapproved of by the Church, has now become widespread. At the point where the priest says that the duty of the wife is to "obey her husband", the bride steps on the bridegroom's toe, signifying her not wholehearted compliance with this. Fortunately, at our Orthodox wedding, my wife didn't understand enough Greek to know when this point arrived!

the seriousness with which Orthodoxy regards marriage. In fact, an Orthodox marriage is not "till death do us part" only but survives in the next world. Thus, although human weakness and our ability to get it wrong is recognized in the Church's reluctant acceptance of divorce and remarriage, these are still relatively rare and it is not that common even for widows or widowers to remarry.

Following the crowning, the couple drink three sips of wine from a common glass as an echo of the Communion Service and a symbol of their common life together. The priest then leads them and the Koumbaros or Koumbara around the table three times, a ritual dance of joy, while the congregation throw rice and flower petals. Since the rice throwing can become a little boisterous, the priest carrying the Gospel often finds the Word of God a literal protection against flying grain! Finally, all three kiss the Gospel to represent their acceptance of the word of God. After a brief sermon from the priest, the couple, Koumbaros or Koumbara and the families line up to receive the greetings and good wishes of the congregation ("Na Zisetai" is the usual greeting). As they leave, the people are given sugared almonds, biscuits and walnuts in honey.

After the wedding, of course, there is the reception. A Greek wedding reception is not for the faint-hearted. They generally last until the early hours of the morning and, while there are no speeches, there is plenty of dancing, drinking and inordinate quantities of food. Course follows course throughout the evening and I would strongly advise fasting before attending a Greek wedding, for the sake of your stomachs rather than any spiritual reasons.

Betrothal the blessing of the rings

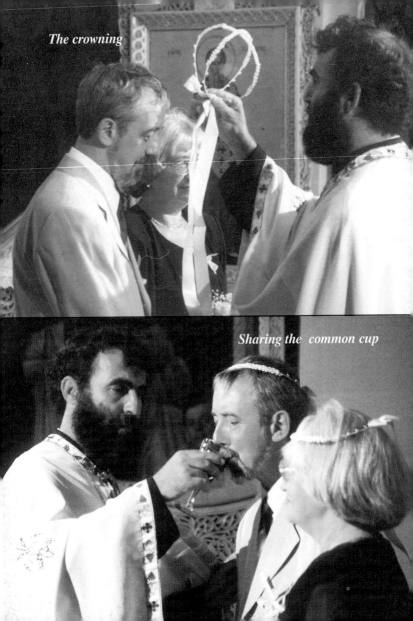

The crowning

Sharing the common cup

The dance of joy

Funerals

For the sake of completeness I must say a word about the less joyful occasions. Feel free to skip this section if you wish. Orthodox Christians have a total belief in life after death and in the ultimate resurrection of the dead. Death is thus a sleep rather than the end. In fact, the English word "cemetery" comes from the Greek "Kimitirio" which literally means "sleeping" place. Thus although funerals are, of course, occasions of grief and mourning, the general tone of the prayers and hymns reflect thanksgiving for the life of the deceased and joyful hope for his or her future glory. At an Orthodox funeral, it is usual to have the coffin open so that the mourners can say their farewells "face to face". The service, as in most Christian denominations takes place in the church and, as the mourners leave, bread and crushed wheat are given out in memory of the departed. This is an echo of the ancient custom whereby alms were distributed to the poor after a funeral. The Greek for "Condolences" is "Silipitiria".

The cortege then proceeds to the cemetery where a further service takes place, final farewells are said and the coffin is closed. In Greece, people are buried in tombs built above ground. After a period of about

3 years, the bones are then exhumed, cleaned and placed in a box which is placed in the ossuary near the cemetery. This is mainly related to the Orthodox belief in the physical resurrection of the body but, especially in the bigger cities, the custom also has a more practical aspect. There simply isn't the space for large, permanent cemeteries*.

Memorial Services

On the third, ninth and fortieth day following a death and on the anniversary, a short memorial service is held, usually at the end of the evening service on Saturday and/or after Holy Communion on Sunday. Prayers are offered for the repose of the departed. Throughout Greece, you will see posters on walls and telegraph poles announcing these "Mnimosyna". Funerals are also announced in the same way, the word to look for being "Kideia".

---

* The Orthodox Church has always been totally opposed to cremation on theological grounds but the issue is not entirely clear and there is quite a lot of discussion going on in the Church at the moment. Certainly, many bishops have accepted the government's proposals to allow cremation for non-Orthodox and there have been influential voices raised within the Church questioning the theological basis for the ban.

The traditional way of notifying funerals
and memorial services can be quicker than the newspaper.

"*Grant* **us** *a* Christian **end**
to our **life**":
places of peace
and repose

Shrines

So what are all those little shrines dotted along the roads of Greece? Since they seem to often appear on dangerous corners, I assumed when I first moved to Greece that they were memorials to fatal accidents. Some of them are in fact just that but the majority are the opposite - thanks offerings to God for lucky escapes*. As mentioned above, people in Greece still build churches to express their thanks for divine assistance and these shrines are a less expensive means of achieving the same object. They range in style from simple boxes with a cross on the top to intricate replicas of churches. Inside, there are icons and a small oil lamp and, if they are memorials, a photograph of the loved one. Whatever their condition or state of repair, please treat shrines with respect - they are religious objects and mean a lot to someone.

---

* *The number and location of these shrines certainly inspire one to drive carefully.*

Simple, grandiose, ornate and even handmade...

roadside Shrines come in a wide range of styles.

ΛPPENDIX ONE

The Byzantine Empire

Although it ended over 500 years ago, the Byzantine Empire is still integral to Greek Orthodoxy because, not only is the "Byzantine style" very important in Greek church architecture, music and icon painting, but most of the major developments in Orthodox theology and liturgical practice occurred during this period. The history of the Byzantine Empire is not widely known in western Europe. Indeed, the adjective "Byzantine" is generally used in a pejorative way to describe an over-complex system of bureaucracy and rigid formalism, coupled with intrigue and murder. And yet, this empire lasted for over a thousand years.

In 330 AD, the Roman emperor Constantine, recently converted to Christianity*, moved his capital from Rome to the Greek city of Byzantium on the Bosphoros, renaming it Constantinople. As the western part of the Empire gradually fell to the ravages of invasion, the Eastern empire became the successor to Rome. Although this empire expanded and contracted during its long history, for long periods it covered the Balkan Peninsular, Asia Minor, Crete, Cyprus and southern Italy. At its furthest extent, in the 6th century, it also included all of Italy, most of North Africa and part of Spain. However, by the 15th century it had been reduced to the area around Constantinople, which finally fell to the Ottoman Turks in 1453, marking the end of the Empire**.

Despite variations in size and occasional incursions by invaders, the structure and administration of the empire remained remarkable stable. The government was highly centralized, with the emperor as absolute ruler. In theory, the senate elected the ruler and the

---

* *St. Constantine is a deeply respected saint in Greece, usually coupled with his mother, St Helen, who played an important role in the spread of Christianity in the Roman Empire.*

** *History and modernity often mingle in strange ways in Greece and all Greeks, even on the TV News, still refer to Istanbul as Constantinople.*

people approved him but, in practice, the oldest son of the emperor usually succeeded to the throne. However, incompetent rulers were often overthrown by revolts and the reputation of Byzantium for plotting and intrigue is not wholly undeserved. The empire was served by a large and efficient civil service and a large, well trained and well equipped army, which together ensured that imperial laws were enforced throughout the empire.

This is not a history book, however, and it is the religious dimension of the Empire that is important for our purpose. The emperor was not only the highest civil power, living in the greatest luxury and wielding almost unlimited power. He was also regarded as a sacred person, God's representative on earth and the protector of Orthodoxy. He had special privileges in the church services* and summoned the great councils of bishops which, over four and a half centuries, established the basic beliefs and practices of Orthodoxy.

In spite of his importance in the Church, the Emperor was clearly defined as the temporal authority only and, in spiritual matters and in the definition and teaching of the faith, the bishops, led by the Pat-

---

The vestments of today's bishops are, in fact those which the emperor would wear in church.

riarch of Constantinople* were supreme. Thus, Church and State formed a unified whole, working in harmony, each supreme in its own sphere. The Byzantine Empire was inspired by a great vision: to establish here on earth a living image of God's government in heaven. "They believed that Christ, who lived on earth as a man, has redeemed every aspect of human existence, and they held that it was therefore possible to baptize not human individuals only but the whole spirit and organization of society. So they strove to create a polity entirely Christian in its principles of government and in its daily life"[7].

Of course, this idealism did not always work out in practice and duplicity, violence and cruelty were all too often the norm. Nevertheless, many of the emperors were genuinely saintly men and during many years of its existence, Byzantium justified its description as "the image of the heavenly Jerusalem". "Religion entered into every aspect of Byzantine life. Byzantine holidays were religious festivals; the races which took place in the Circus began with the singing of hymns; and trade contracts invoked the Trinity and were marked with

_____

* *Still regarded as the spiritual leader of the Orthodox Church, the Patriarch of Constantinople is also head of the Church in Crete and parts of northern Greece.*

the sign of the Cross. Today, in an untheological age, it is all but impossible to realize how burning an interest was felt in religious questions by every part of society, by laity as well as clergy, by the poor and uneducated as well as the Court and scholars"[8].

The Byzantine dream of government and spirit united in a single sanctified state still represents to Orthodox a symbol of the "new Heaven and new earth" which all Christians believe is the ultimate end of human existence. In more practical ways, Byzantium was central to the formulation and clarification of Orthodox dogma, the exterior forms of the churches, the development of icon painting, the music* and even most of the vestments worn by the clergy. The liturgies which we celebrate today were written during the Byzantine period and the language of all services is Byzantine Greek rather than modern Greek. Although there have been developments and changes in the Orthodox Church over the centuries, in most instances, we worship today using the same words and rituals written and defined by St. Basil the Great and St. John Chrysostom in the 4th century.

---

* *Even the music of "demotika" - Greek folk songs - derives from the music of Byzantine hymns.*

191

Byzantium - Church and state united:
Emperors Constantine and Justinian offer
the city to Christ and the Virgin Mary.

The Church of Holy Wisdom (St. Sofia), Constantinople

The Three Hierarchs, St. Basil the Great, St. John Chrysostom and St. Gregory, formulated much of the theology and liturgy of Orthodoxy.

ΛPPENDIX TWO

The Byzantine Greek Alphabet

All icons show the name of the saint or description of the event depicted. The following notes and alphabet may help you decipher the more common.

- The word for saint is "Agios" (male) or "Agia" (female) often abbreviated to "Ag".
- "Ο ΩΝ". This is the name God gives himself in the Old Testament ("The I Am")* and is obligatory on all icons of Christ, usually written in the halo.

---

* *See Exodus 3,14 "And God said unto Moses, I AM THAT I AM"*

- "ICXC" is the abbreviated name of Jesus Christ (ΙΗΣΟΥΣ ΧΡΙΣΤΟC), found on all icons of Christ.
- "MP ΘΥ" stands for "MHTHP ΘΕΟΥ" (Mother of God), one of the titles given to the Virgin Mary. These letters are found on all icons of Mary.

Although the alphabet used is basically the same as modern Greek, there are some difficulties. The main problem is that often two letters are blended together or one may be written above the other. However, with a little practice, you will soon get the hang of it.

Greek Alphabet		English Alphabet		Greek Alphabet	
A	α	*a*	*n*	N	ν
B	β	*v*	*x*	Ξ	ξ
Γ	γ	*g,y*	*o*	O	ο
Δ	δ	*d*	*p*	Π	π
E	ε	*e*	*r*	P	ϱ
Z	ζ	*z*	*s*	C	σ
H	η	*i*	*t*	T	τ
Θ	θ	*th*	*u*	Y	υ
I	ι	*i*	*f, ph*	Φ	φ
K	χ	*k*	*ch*	X	χ
Λ	λ	*l*	*ps*	Ψ	ψ
M	μ	*m*	*o*	Ω	ω

ΛPPENDIX THREE

Name Days

The names listed below are only the more common Greek names and variations. I have listed them according to their "Sunday names", i.e. the full saint's name, followed by diminutives, male/female equivalents and English equivalents where appropriate.

Gr.			*En.*	
Andreas			Andrew	30 *Nov.*
Anna			Ann	25 *July or* 9 *Dec.*
Despina	Despo			15 *Aug.*
Dimitrios	Dimitris, Mimis	Dimitra		26 *Oct.*

Gr.			*En.*	
Ekaterini	Katerina		Catherine	25 *Nov.*
Eleni			Helen	21 *May*
Emmanouil	Manos, Manolis	Emmanuella	Emmanuel	25 *Dec.*
Evangelos	Vangelis	Evangelia		25 *March*
Giorgos		Georgia	George	23 *April*[a]
Ilias		Iliana	Elijah	20 *July*
Ioannis	Iannis	Ioanna	John	7 *Jan.* or 24 *June*
Irini	Rena		Irene	5 *May*
Konstantinos	Kostas, Dino	Konstantina	Constantine	21 *May*
Maria	Maro	Marios	Mary	15 *Aug.*[b]
Michail	Michalis		Michael	8 *Nov.*[c]
Nikolaos	Nikos	Nikoletta	Nicholas	6 *Dec.*[d]
Panagiotis	Panos	Panagiota	Lit. All Holy	15 *Aug.*[e]
Sofia			Sophia	17 *Sep.*
Stavros		Stavroula	Lit. The Cross	14 *Sep.*
Vasilios	Vasili	Vasilia	Basil	1 *Jan.*

a) 23 April frequently falls during Lent and, if this happens, the name day, along with any others that occur during the fast, is celebrated on the Monday or Tuesday after Easter.

b) This is the name day for married Maria's; unmarried girls called Maria often celebrate on 21 November.

c) The Archangel Michael is regarded as the protector of airmen, so this is also the "name-day" of the Air Force.

d) Also the "name-day" of the Navy as St. Nicholas is the protector of sailors.

e) One of the appellations of the Virgin Mary.

ὁ ΑΡΧ

ΜΙΧΑΛ

A few **more** *of the* Host *of* Heaven

St. Michael, the Archangel.

(right p.) St. George, patron saint of the army

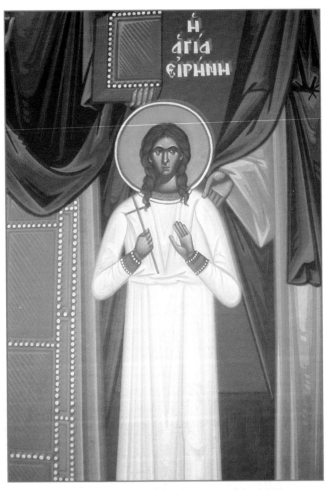

St. Irini, a 12 year old girl, martyred in 1463.

Ο ΑΓΙΟΣ   ΔΗΜΗΤΡΙΟΣ

St. Dimitros, patron saint of Thessaloniki.

Ἡ ἉΓΙΑ ΑΙΚΑΤΕΡΙΝΗ

The Prophet Elijah (Ilias)
(left p.) **St. Catherine with the instrument of her torture and death**

Ο ΑΓΙΟΣ

ΑΝΔΡΕ
ΑΣ
Ο ΠΡΩΤΟΚΛΗΤΟΣ

St. Andrew

Further Reading

If your interest has been aroused and you want more detail about the beliefs and practices of Orthodoxy, I strongly recommend "The Orthodox Church" by Timothy Ware (Bishop Kallistos) published by Penguin Books. It is a highly readable account of the history, beliefs and worship of the Orthodox Church by a man widely acknowledged as the leading contemporary Orthodox theologian.

In spite of its rather solemn title, "The Theology of the Icon" by Leonid Ouspensky is actually quite approachable and gives a clear outline of the symbolism of icons and the history of icon painting. You may be interested to know that the Archbishop of Canterbury, Rowan Williams, has just published a book on icons of the Virgin Mary called " Ponder These Things".

"For the Life of the World" by Alexander Schmemann is somewhat deeper and a little dry in parts but is an excellent introduction to the sacraments and worship in the Orthodox Church.

If you are interested in history, the Oxford History of Byzantium, published in 2003, received excellent reviews although I have not had a chance to read it myself yet.

Most of the services of the Orthodox Church are available in English translation, including the services of Holy Week, weddings and baptisms.

For any books about Orthodoxy, I can only recommend Orthodox Christian Books of Newcastle - under - Lyme (Telephone 01782576933). It is not a bookshop as such but does offer a mail order retail service. Nicholas and Nina Chapman are extremely friendly and are always willing to offer help and advice.

And finally - I hope you have enjoyed this book but I am all too aware of its limitations. In spite of checks by two theologians, I am sure there are still errors or gaps. Indeed, my publishers can confirm that I was still making additions and corrections during the final proof reading! So, if you have any other questions or comments I would be pleased to hear from you.

NOTES

1   Ware   (*page* 269)

2   Ware   (*page* 234)

3   Anglican Book of Common Prayer

4   Ware   (*page* 271)

5   Quoted in Ouspensky (*page* 37)

6   Quoted in Ware (*page* 273)

7   Ware   (*page* 42)

8   Ware   (*page* 35)